# Eternal...

## Like the Galaxy

JANHVI KHOSHE

Writer's Pocket

First published by Writer's Pocket in 2023

email: publish@writerspocket.com



ISBN-13: 978-93-6083-446-3



www.writerspocket.com

*This Book is dedicated to*

*Aai and Baba,*
*The most supportive duo of my life.*

# Preface

Poetry as a medium has resonated with me a lot since childhood. I have been inspired, felt understood and been advised by poetries at times. Even though I wrote poetries as a child, I understood more about the art of expression during my teen years. I had been a part of drama/theater for a long period of time, through which I understood how the words in which your characters express are of utmost importance before you even get into the nuances of facial expressions and performances.

As a theater artist and a fellow human being, I felt strongly about certain situations and emotions, for which I used poetry as a medium of expression. This collection encompasses the poetries that I have written over a period of time, when I was passing through different phases of my life.

As our emotional reactions and mental perceptions change over time, we look at topics differently because we outgrow our previous thoughts. Similarly, the poetries that you will read in this collection which have been written by me from when I was a teenager to this very year, differ in their expression. The only aspect that remains constant is my immense hunger for expressing my heart.

# CONTENTS

# The right person

# 1. The right person

The right person will take you from the arid forests to
the dynamic galaxies filled with love and contentment
They will always see the wonderful art that you are and
you won't find the need to wear those expensive clothes
or watches to impress them...

You have some charming aspects, some flaws as well
and they'll see them all,
But the reason why they'll decide to stay is that it'll be
no one else but 'you'

The right person will never compare you to some
stranger who appears to be cool on social media,
Instead, they'll appreciate the beauty you've added to
their life!

They'll not just add wings to your plane but will also be
your copilot in the journeys ahead...
For them, your company will matter more than
materialistic gifts, and the time spent with you will
always act as the best therapy!

Even when you might have a rough day at work, you'll
find them sitting next to you, ready to give you a
listening ear...

And if you ever feel you've lost your spark, you wouldn't have to look anywhere else but just into their eyes,
Because for the right person, there'll be no star brighter than the one shining right in front of them!

**My smile will be brighter than yours**

## 2. My smile will be brighter than yours

Maybe because I don't think of tit for tat
while giving
I tend to give wholeheartedly,
My wishes, my prayers, my emotions
To the dear ones...

I know your journey is purely yours, if you work hard,
you'll achieve everything
But if you don't, you'll have to turn back
and alter the age-old methods,
And the same is true for me
But how can I make those thrifty wishes for you and the
gigantic ones for me?
I've got to be extravagant because my Soul desires to be

The beaming sunshine, that I ever feel is through the
love, through the light, through the wellness of the
people around me
And I've always been ready to hold your hand while
you're paving your way towards the dawn,
And I'll be there as an invisible genie to make sure you
stay happy

I'll never leave you during the entire journey,
Underneath the bright stars, we'll stand knowing that
you'll shine like one of them soon

And I know that after those efforts,
When you finally succeed
I'll be standing right behind you

Whether you look at me or not
My heart will be beaming with joy
Looking at your success, looking at you finally achieve your goals, looking at those tender wings ready to soar high in the sky

And at that moment I'll find
what I always imagined
My smile to be brighter than yours…

# A Peek into the Soul

# 3. A Peek into the Soul

The glitter on my dress,
The scarf around my neck
The Taylor Swift songs on my playlist.
And my 20-slided PowerPoint deck

Feel pretty much like a modern woman
Trying to ace it all
But these taglines come from around me
In the traps of modernity I fall

As modern as I might dress
And cool beverages I might sip
My mind flies back to the period of Jane Austen
Wondering if it's possible to take back a trip

Pretty letters I want to write
And attend a wholesome ball dance
As my gowns bejeweled with flamboyance be ready
I'd be eager to meet another artist in France

The time around seems dull today
Where aesthetic is just for reels
What happened to intelligent poetry
Replaced with "#Sundayfeels"

My mind is not just ready
For the labels given to me
For As perspectives change so might I
Even if I choose the eyes who see

But I'm not who you think I am
Nor am I what I feel
It's this journey called life that takes
For this startling reveal

At the end, it's the soul that we try to keep at peace
It doesn't know the perfect way
And the reason I think of this so much
Is that it finds its light some day

# Beautiful Women

# 4. Beautiful Women

She is one of the most beautiful women
I've seen
Yet you'll never see her on a ramp
She has never worn glittery gowns
But when it comes to horse riding, she's an absolute champ
Her sister who is a talented fashionista, who always carries her make-up kit, whose dark burgundy lip gloss and perfectly curled hair are well stylized, is equally pretty!

When I pen down my poetry,
Never do I ever feel like penning down female characters in ways like above!
I'd rather describe them as kind, artistic, fierce, soft, brave, empathetic, wild and all of them will still be "Beautiful!"
Their external appearances don't matter and can be left up to the readers for imagining...
Because you will see Beauty the way you feel it within!

Being a woman gives me tremendous pleasure in portraying female characters as the most incredible gems ever.

They might transform in a different shape,
Their forms and colors will differ
But no matter what, they'll keep Shining!
And you cannot hide them, not anymore
Because they're the light we need to brighten our worlds, especially on a new moon!

# The Burning Candle

# 5. The Burning Candle

I came home after playing in the sun
And was very tired indeed
Immediately told mom to give me water
Instead she prepared some fresh lemonade

The week after that I had my final exams
Told her to sleep since I had studies to finish
She sat beside me reading magazines
And told me she isn't awake because of me, but to read
instead

The next month we had a party hosted
for my birthday
She prepared the guest list,
made all the arrangements,
told dad to get the decorations required
And made sure I enjoyed to the fullest

The year after that,
I was going through my teen years!
Got pissed at mom when she tried to advice
too much
Said I didn't need any of it
She smiled even then and said, "You'll recall all that I'm
saying someday and will find it useful"

10 years down the line
She still makes sure to look after the house, cook the most amazing meals, make the most practical decisions
And says "I don't like cake anyway you have it"
When there's that last piece left on the plate!

While I know she's always going to be there for me, I wonder how much have I done to let her know I'll be there too!
While she knows my favorite food, color, movie, restaurant, I struggle to find out whether she ever prepares the vegetables of her choice Or even expects us to know them?
Throughout these years, making sure that her family is happy, she sometimes forgets she's not just a mom or a wife
She's a human!
Human from whom we expect
too much sometimes,
Human who has a heart just like ours,
Human who gets tired and sadly,
Human who is not as adorned as other professionals by the vice of being taken for granted
I don't think she expects anything in return

But one day if you take some extra effort to get to know her a little better just like you do with your other friends,
You'll know that she's the candle that makes sure there's never any darkness around
Meanwhile, we forget: In the process, she's burning too!

# On the other Side of the spectrum

# 6. On the other Side of the spectrum

I took some time to review a
throwback yesterday
While turning the pages of my photo album,
I met a person
She looked quite familiar
She reminded me of someone
Smiled just like me, her curls rolled up and her cheeks
both chubby

But some things were different…

Her eyes shone with a different spark
Hiding the questions of insecurity
Insecurities about the future
She was a nice child perhaps,
Felt as if she was waiting for someone
To show her the world
To calm her mind
And to tell her that future is a surprise,
don't get so anxious

Despite those tangled emotions, she seemed ready to
take up adventures
She was eccentric but sweet

She was no one else but my younger self

But somehow, I thought,
I didn't know her anymore,
The perplexed looking child no longer existed
She had grown into a different woman,
who had left her insecurities somewhere along the journey
Who had learnt to smile unconditionally
Her eyes still shone bright, but with the peace that came from within

And while turning the last page, the last image, the younger one smiled nervously and uttered softly:
"Maybe the art itself doesn't know how beautiful it's going to be until you finish that last stroke!
I shut the album peacefully whispering to her
"I'll meet you on the other side of the mystery and trust me it will look prettier than you imagined"

# A self-woven story?

# 7. A self-woven story?

Life........ Is a story!
Story whose last para is yet to be written!
If I handover the pen to you
(you're just waiting for the opportunity, aren't you?),
you exactly know how to make it tragic!

I have woven the words so beautifully till now,
that any reader is going to be enticed by their beauty,
and I have made sure of it!

There are parts of this story that might go unnoticed
But for anyone who's got a little more patience to seek through,
will get to know its purity

I've heard about your writing skills!
You've got beautiful stories by your side and I don't doubt them!
But the difference between the stories you write and my story is: Honesty

I live my story, then present it and you present your story first and then act like that's the way it happened!

And if we talk about the readers,
they may get wrongly informed at times,
But you never accept it and I never mind
Because I love my story and I value it as much as I should!

Many suggested I hand over the task of "writing the climax" to you!

But this is my story peer.

Yes, I'm definitely trying to portray the most exemplary character!
And handing over the pen to you simply means handing over this universe full of wonders to you!

So how ever my story might be, crazy, eccentric, or bold,
I'm sure it's never going to be fictitious just to attract an audience!
And deep inside, even you know that honesty has its own stature!

# The answer is YOU

## 8. The answer is YOU

I go to school, I come from school
I have good days, some bad days, and some days, I just have to face it all.

But all the turmoil that goes in my mind
day after day,
Comes to a standstill every night
before I go to bed...
Always wondered about how this happens,
why this happens
But the so-called anonymous answer seems to have been in front of me

It all falls back into place just by looking at your smile,
Listening to the sounds of positivity pouring right out of your heart!
You're possibly the only star who keeps shining just for me
Am I so busy to notice that the answer has been right there?
That I have been so blind to observe the little efforts you take every day to comfort my heart?
I'd just say that I wouldn't grow to become this person without you,
Mom!

# Everyone needs that one person

## 9. Everyone needs that one person

Everyone needs that one person, who makes you a little
more strong
Even if problems arise
they don't let you do wrong

Everyone needs that one person who tries to give you
everything
May it be a grand surprise or as small as a flower like
thing

Everyone needs that one person who cares for you more
than themself
Who shape your life in a way that they try to make it
more beautiful

And everyone needs that one person, who after you,
Make your life theirs and try to live it with full
conviction

Everyone might be gifted with such a person in their
lives,
It might be their mom, dad, friend
or any well-wisher!
But if you expect to have such a person
in your life,
First you have to be that person
For someone or even your own self!

# The Embellished Garden

## 10. The Embellished Garden

The chirpy birds in my garden
Still sing the gleeful song
To keep me more blissful at work
From dusk until the dawn

I have lovely memories woven around this place
They're always good enough to bring a smile on my face

I look back to see again
Those knots that once I tied
Just like the boulevard near my house
Whose shrubs perhaps have dried

For you were busy looking at the sun,
Didn't see the chaos behind
Yet the reason I didn't say anything
Today seems satisfying

But in the years coming forth
Those efforts will be worthwhile
For I know this land of sentiments
Is still much fertile

It might not have the flowers that once adorned its way
But some tulips filled with kindness instead are enough
to make my day

I just want to say again
To the seeds that once I sowed
When you'll turn into pretty little flowers
You'll find me on the same road

And even in the times
When about the shredding leaves you mourn
I'll be sitting right next to you
Picking your each and every thorn

For promises that I make
Will never go unkept
And I'll always try to keep my garden
The most beautiful and perfect.

# Fading in Oblivion

## 11. Fading in Oblivion

"It is time to keep moving ahead",
they exclaimed
But I wanted to take a halt
I waited for the darkness to fade away
For the dawn to Arrive
For the beam of sunlight
to finally seep into my eyes
I waited and waited
But, no sign of any miracle to happen!

Too tired, when I finally stepped out to see,
They were all there, the sunrays, light and dawn it was!!
"What an unworldly obscurity?'' I exclaimed

And then someone affirmed, "Very fair!
For darling, life this is,
Here you don't wait for your turn to come,
You just grab your pass, enter the game, make your
move, steal that limelight,
And finally when you're done with your journey, even
the grave in which you're laid in,
feels your weight,
Weight of your achievements, weight of your
eccentricities, weight of those dark struggles and rising
from them!!

Because this is how it has to be played!!
For if waiting is all you do, you end **Unrecognized**!"

# Finding your bliss

## 12. Finding your bliss

Maybe the reason why we experience the burden of
unhealthy emotions
Is the futuristic complex expectation of happiness!

But do the complex things which encompass
materialism, make us happy?
If happiness is intangible, it has to come from intangible
assets!

The little things such as observing
the weather around,
Looking at a little kid narrate what happened on the first
day of her school,
Having a cup of coffee whilst reading poetry,
Calling up a close friend for a conversation,
Or even singing a song when no one's listening can give
us the soothing feeling which we experience when a cold
breeze touches our face in hot summers!!

In the end, what we realize is that instead of waiting for
someone or something to come running to us and
surprise us with the gift called 'happiness,'

It's always better to create our own green garden that
can be grown the way we want to by sowing the seeds of
'our' favorite flowers

Meanwhile, philosophy says the more you give the more you receive

Or sometimes you're so involved in giving that you don't realize what you're getting in return is 10 times more than you give…

# The Halfwit Mind of Mine

## 13. The Halfwit Mind of Mine

Oh, I had been such a halfwit!
I considered the times of bitter sobs and fragile emotions
to last forever

While learning to live with eccentricities,
The ones which dreaded my days,
There walked in a person one day
Who made it all go away

There was a listening ear, a melting touch, and a
heartwarming smile that arose,
She packed them all, the dejection, despair, the nervous
gloomy blows
Oh, how she'd known to dispose of this junk which was
just so insolvent...
For Mother, how I wish I had known, you were the only
one who could have rescued me from this "torment!"

# To my future daughter...

# 14. To my future daughter…

Hello Manu,
How's it on the other side?
Intriguing? Beautiful?

I never said that there'll be a bed of roses
in front of you,
I don't want you to think of life that way
Just want you to learn to pave your way through the
thorns slowly and steadily
While you hold one of my hands
for the initial support

I don't want you to have it all figured so soon
But instead would love it if you smile while you're
making sense of your circumstances

I don't expect you to be one of those kids who feature on
Little Big shots
Instead, I would value the very fact that you're my little
big shot
Who is kind enough to care about the people in her little
world

I don't care if you can play games on my smartphone
when you're just four

But I'd encourage you to dive as deep as you can in a
book that you just picked from my library rack.

I don't expect you to get an A+ in math,
I'd rather motivate you to look beyond that 'A' and
always look at your bigger
picture for the future

I'd want you to learn
I'd want you to explore
But most importantly, I'd want you to fall in love with
the beautiful person that you are

And though I can't hide the realities of this world from
you,
I'll make sure I give you better sunglasses,
Through which you see different perspectives,
A few glimpses of my perspectives...

And while you see the good in others,
Never forget to appreciate the greener grass in your
garden and the flowers which make it more beautiful!

# My heart is too small

# 15. My heart is too small

Sometimes I feel that we're not different people
Instead, similar people on different journeys!

And it's not the journey that keeps me afar
but my heart!
Imagine fitting China lights in a glass jar
As beautiful as they look,
They can never replace the calmness that your eyes feel
by looking at the stars in the night sky flashing for you...

My love for you or 'You' in fact are like the night sky
filled with stars

But I can never fit you or my feelings in a tiny glass jar!
Nor can I use words to describe them because words
might never be able to encompass the depth of my
emotions!
So instead of worrying about encapsulating you in my
tiny heart,
I'd rather let you be where you are and look at you shine
from a distance!

For I know,
When the sky shines because of the stars,
A part of us always gets illuminated by its light,
No matter how far we are from it, physically!

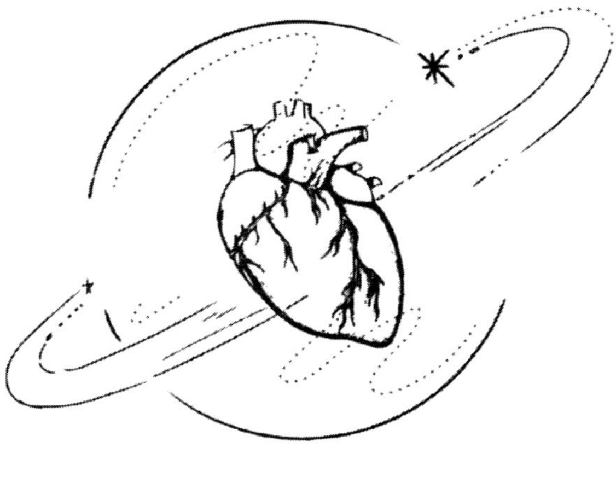

Similarly, I brighten up by your happiness and your shining persona
Looking at you from places where you can't find me,
But I will be there for you
As long as there's night sky and my eyes are open to see it!

# Our Galaxies

## 16. Our Galaxies

When the moon sets into its den today
And the sun rises to brighten your curtain drapes
I hope for once you look outside,
Just like your heart, you'll see me escape

My stars might not align with your stars
My mind won't be in the same place as yours
But as long as the lining of our souls align
I know every genuine emotion will endure

I try to contain the thoughts that go haywire
Their destination is your name
I better train them to look beyond you
Because I know I'd lose this game

As the sky above me has no end
So does the entangled spirit trying to free from your thread
And since I believe in an afterlife
I'd imagine being united with you there instead

Because we both reside in galaxies far apart
Where your hue is somewhat new
But the one thing I would never want you to forget
Is that I created a new star in my galaxy and named it after YOU!

# Being my own Moon

# 17. Being my own Moon

I'll write celestial poems for you,
Place you next to my favorite moon,
Talk about your shining eyes and soulful words
Turn around with a beaming face, everytime that I hear your voice!

Admire nothing but you, your eyes and your blissful presence!
Standing in front of the mirror, 'your' soul is what I feel
I don't have enough adjectives to describe myself, because for you I have used most of them

But...

Why don't I ever see myself in there?
While I smile, while I turn, should I love myself equally if not more than you, just for once?
Should I remind myself to shout out at my achievements a little louder just as I do for yours?
While I look at the stars, should I see myself as one of them just as I like to see you?
Should I walk with myself under the rain without you being beside me?

Should I finally accept, that it's new moon and you've risen with your charming presence elsewhere?
Should I finally unweave myself from your silver coated knots and create my own galaxy?

I think I should!

And if I do so, this time, I'll not be looking for another
moon to write about
But be that moon myself...
Flaunting my dark patches as some of my costliest
possessions!

# The twinkling Star

## 18. The twinkling Star

She stands upright on the floor, wearing a dazzling
purple gown, her hair clipped and tucked behind her ear,
She's not sure whether she's ready,
She's not sure whether her eyes reflect the exact
emotions that are present within her

She looks down, at the glass floor
Takes a closer look at her reflection...
She looks like the girl she wanted to be,
That girl who only existed in her imaginary story until
now

Story that she had created 10 years ago
in her mind
But she was not sure whether she could
really be that girl

And suddenly she feels a jolt,
Jolt from her inner self
For all those insecurities gushing through her heart,
severe than they ever were,
And this was not the time to make the buzzing bees of
self-doubt hover around,

All those negative bits had their days in the past,
They were done telling her about how incapable she
was,

how no one would look at her bright side,
how no one would ever hear her out and how
she was not the star that could twinkle

But today is not that day

As she takes a deep breath and looks right up
She can see all those connoisseurs
And they are looking at her,
Their cheerful faces beaming,

Suddenly she realizes that it all actually existed within
her
She was ready
This time she truly was
She raised her mic and let the emotions flow,
From the low notes to the high,
From the subtle sways to those impromptu
hand gestures
And she could nail them all,

And maybe this time she had to accept that her eyes did
shine,
Brighter than she ever thought they could
And that's when they all knew, the star was ready to
'twinkle'!!

**I wish we could fly back to last October**

# 19. I wish we could fly back to last October

How I wish we could fly back to the last October
When the air was much purer, the sky was much brighter
and we were filled with more love than we are today

Last October has truly been the best of its kind.
It has seen more of my love, more of my fears,
more of your happiness, more of your eccentricities,
and more of my never-ending chirping!

It has given us memories we would never want to untie from our hats
We'll be living our lives with a reminiscence of these details
And wish we celebrated them while we lived them, in the years coming forth
But how I wish we had been informed earlier, that our last October was parting to never meet us again...

# Not yet the star I want to be

## 20. Not yet the star I want to be

When the glitter looked too far away
I assumed maybe it was not my day

While celebrations were at peak,
And the crackers lit the sky
I just sat down like a bird injured
Who despite its wings could not fly

The air around was gloomy
My eyes as dry as thorns
Didn't know that the bird I thought I was
Would never be well adorned

Then suddenly heard a voice
Who urged me to look behind
The nest from where I had started flying
Was nowhere for me to find!

I remembered the bright shine
That was always present in my eye
The 'little me' saw dreams of flying away
No matter how far was the sky

Then knew that more than other stars,
I was the one being tested
As the pole star I was meant to be,
I would shine brighter than expected!

# Being YOUR Best

# 21. Being YOUR Best

Did I just hear Ria wanting to be the number one athlete
in the world?
And John the best pianist!
Rita wanting to amuse the world with
her designs
And Saniya trying to solve the 400-year-old math
problem?

Well some of them if not all, want to be number one to
be remembered!
But...

What if I choose to look at this differently?
If Narain is not the kindest person in the world, but
perhaps gave 'you' a call on your sad days, would you
not remember him?
If Kabir is not the best cook in the world, but served you
food on your starving day, wouldn't you be grateful?
If Anu is not a billionaire but helps the little
impoverished kids to go to school, would her efforts be
forgotten?
And if I as a stranger extended help in times of utter
chaos, wouldn't I pop up in your head
even once?

You perhaps do not have to be the best in the
world/region for people to remember you!
You can just be the best 'You'

You can just do the best work you've ever done,
Paint your best Canvas,
Sing your best song
Or just understand your presence and its meaning for people around you!

If my comparison was with someone else
I'd have to wait for victory till eternity for there might always be someone better

But since my comparison is with 'my' own self,
I can celebrate my triumph any day
As long as I have the will and determination to shape the best-ever sculpture out of me!

# Wrapped Warrior

## 22. Wrapped Warrior

You think it's going to be good
When you quit that task you love to do just because it's tough

When you decide to let go of your
most awaited challenge
because it demands a lot of your
creativity and sweat
When you know you want to achieve your fitness goals
But giving up seems an easier option than doing 30 burpees a day

You think these adverse reasons for comforting yourself
are the only cookies you need at the moment
And tomorrow when you see your own neighbor run a
21 km marathon, which once was on your bucket list,
you soothe yourself by saying her life's just easier than mine

When you see that guy from your class bag
those decoration contracts you've always
dreamt of,
You know there's some part missing from your life decor
But you narrow your thoughts down by saying
He's just gotten lucky

Yes you can explain yourself a million times about how
your life has bigger challenges than others and that your
comfort matters,

But amidst all this, have you totally forgotten about the
happiness and satisfaction you get by saying 'I finally
did it?'

That feeling is incomparable
It's enormous than your struggles,
Than that sweet lie you keep telling yourself about how
everyone else can achieve their goals
except for 'you'

Just for once awaken the warrior inside, who's wrapped
in the bubble wrap of solace!
It's time to unwrap them
To greet them with a cheerful 'Hello'
And finally years later, when you'll be taking your
evening stroll in the park,
Another wrapped warrior might get influenced by your
journey and think
'Here's the person who (no matter how challenging their
ride was), just did not give up!'

# A Masterpiece

## 23. A Masterpiece

Have you ever looked at a sculpture/monument and been awestruck?
No comments, no words
just completely transfixed?
I have been,
Many times, in fact…
So much that I've started comparing it
to Life itself

While sculpting any piece of art, its foundation carries utmost importance
Because the foundation is what forms the core of the piece
Similarly, our upbringing, childhood experiences and opportunities are monumental in deciding what kind of path we are going to follow

But is that it?

Not really

Consider the foundation to be rock solid
But it has its status intact until we build the whole structure

After the entire sculpture is complete and polished, the final outcome is what is going to be viewed,
That is what is going to decide the overall look of the piece

It is going to get all sorts of reviews and praises,
And when that happens, the foundation
suddenly gets de-focused

Our trajectory is exactly the same
We might have done great things in the past,
Or even not so great ones
However, if the past is what we see at every point, the
future growth might get stunted
Also, for the wisest humans ever, the present is what has
always played the role of a game changer

Everything is interconnected on this unique path
And I don't want the sculpture of my life to look
beautiful just because I fear the critics
and their reviews
But because when I look at it from a third persons'
perspective,
I want to be just as awestruck as I am today
When I look at the other masterpieces

# A free verse for what you call fictitious

## 24. A free verse for what you call fictitious

When I'm happy, I look at the sky
When I'm finally able to accomplish an arduous task, I smile looking at the sky
Though fictitious, I think it looks at me too
With a thumbs up

So dear sky,
I think you understand me
Because you see me taking different actions everyday
That's why I think
Though I have people around me,
Though they mostly know what's going on inside me,
And though they're the special ones,
You've got all that positivity and charisma...
Because they know me,
But you "see" me
Every single day.

And when I've been through a gloomy day in autumn, you too become silent,
Trying to figure things out
As if you had been a part of me
And then some ask, "Why are you so fond of inanimate things?"
They might be inanimate for you
For me they're real, My people
Who I know for a fact are my biggest supporters
Forever

Till that last breath I take beneath them

In Fact, I visualize the entire universe observing me sometimes,
Just like a mother looks at her child walking for the first time
That kind of happiness resides inside them!
The moon, stars, and the infinite sky

And they are all my friends
Friends who are meant to stay
Friends who smile when I smile
Friends who emphasize more on teaching me through their changing phases
On how to remain the stronger one
And Friends who keep reminding me that just like us, you too will shine one Day
If that's the kind of treasure I've found, would you still want me to invest in the ones who come in just to leave?
I've learned this, the ones who are meant to stay, are your true ones
And I've found my true ones
Perhaps years later when I grow old and would be gardening in my backyard, I'd look at the sky and think,
"Because of you I didn't give up
Because I always knew that my goal lay in 'touching' you."
And I know the sky will smile even at that time, just like it does today
With a thumbs up and a tiny star by its side, winking right back at me.

# An Artist's Art

## 25. An Artist's Art

We all look at Art and appreciate its beauty
Asking the artist how they come up with such an
immaculate creation!

The artist just smiles looking at you,
hiding all the messy patterns they discarded and
reviewed before presenting
the final master piece!

You love to know where their inspiration comes from
And the answer to that is not that simple...
Sometimes it's from a serene beach where they sit at
night observing the stars,
Sometimes it's from the troubles they've been through
along the way,
Sometimes it's from the tender spark of love that lights
in the corner of their heart
And sometimes from the amalgamation of thoughts
running in their minds with conclusions unknown

The galaxies we talk about in Astro-physics actually
exist in an artist's mind,
They feel it, wonder about the same
But don't necessarily flaunt it

And that's why I believe that Artists are an Art in themself
Just tell that to them once and you will see the dew drops in their work present right in their eyes.

## Writer's Pocket

Writer's Pocket is a publication house established in 2016. We began with the aim of providing a better publishing platform for aspiring writers and budding poets.

The publishing industry in India (and around the world, to a great extent) is always something of a mystery even to the writers themselves. We are working on making publishing more accessible to everyone.

So far, we have helped over 3,000 writers turn their dreams into reality by publishing the books and continue to do so. By doing so, we also provide some of the best content by Indian writers to the readers.

Want to read more books? Scan this QR code with your smartphone and check out all our books on Amazon.